WYOMING

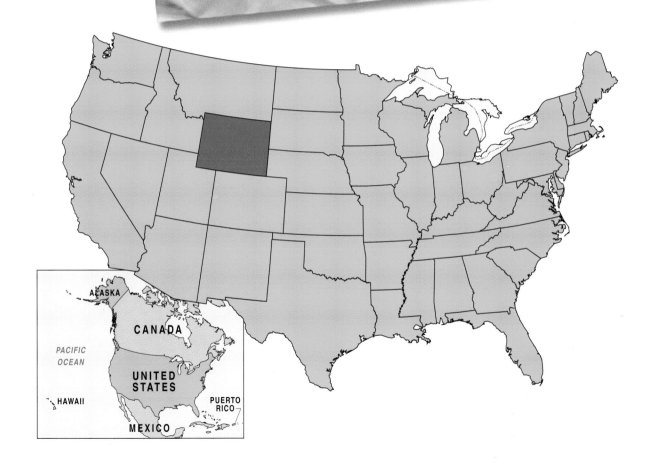

WYOMING

HELLO
U.S.A.

by Carlienne Frisch

Lerner Publications Company

You'll find this picture of jade at the beginning of each chapter in this book. Nephrite, the variety of jade shown here, has been the state gemstone of Wyoming since 1967. Nephrite can be found in a variety of colors, but dark green is the most valuable. Wyoming and Alaska are the only two states where nephrite has been found.

Cover (left): Devils Tower near Hulett. Cover (right): Wild mustangs. Pages 2–3: Yellowstone Falls in Yellowstone National Park. Page 3: Children at Wind River Indian Reservation.

Copyright © 2003 by Lerner Publications Company

This book is available in two editions:
Library binding by Lerner Publications Company, a division of Lerner Publishing Group
Soft cover by First Avenue Editions, an imprint of Lerner Publishing Group
241 First Avenue North
Minneapolis, MN 55401 U.S.A.

Website address: www.lernerbooks.com

Library of Congress Cataloging-in-Publication Data

Frisch, Carlienne, 1944–
   Wyoming / by Carlienne Frisch (Rev. and expanded 2nd ed.)
     p. cm. — (Hello U.S.A.)
   Includes bibliographical references and index.
   Summary: An introduction to the geography, history, economy, people,
    environmental issues, and interesting sites of Wyoming.
   ISBN: 0–8225–4089–4 (lib. bdg. : alk paper)
   ISBN: 0–8225–0799–4 (pbk. : alk paper)
   1. Wyoming—Juvenile literature. [1. Wyoming.] I. Title. II. Series.
  F761.3.F75 2003
  978.9—dc21
                                                 2001007213

Manufactured in the United States of America
1 2 3 4 5 6 – JR – 08 07 06 05 04 03

CONTENTS

The jagged Pilot Peak juts into the sky over the Shoshone National Forest in northwestern Wyoming. Shoshone was the first national forest in the United States.

THE LAND

On the Plains

Wyoming is one of six Rocky Mountain states located in the western United States. It is the ninth largest state in the country. Wyoming stretches from Idaho and Utah on the west to South Dakota and Nebraska on the east. Montana is Wyoming's northern neighbor. Colorado and a corner of Utah border Wyoming on the south.

Wyoming takes its name from *mechewea-mi-ing,* an Indian phrase that means "on the great plains" or "at the big plains." The phrase refers to Wyoming's Great Plains—one of the state's two major land regions.

Visitors to Wyoming might be lucky enough to encounter a herd of buffalo.

7

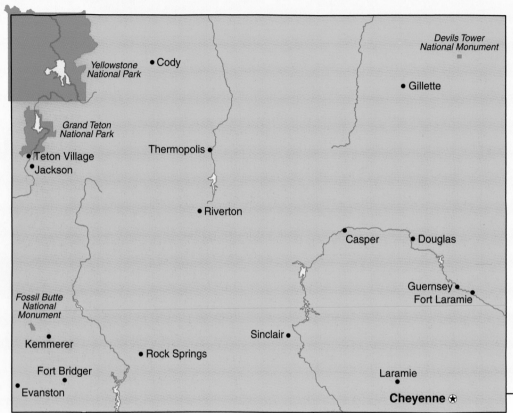

Devils Tower
National Monument ▪

● Gillette

Yellowstone
National Park

● Cody

Grand Teton
National Park

● Teton Village
● Jackson

Thermopolis ●

● Riverton

Casper ●   ● Douglas

Guernsey ●●
Fort Laramie

Fossil Butte
National
Monument

Sinclair ●

Kemmerer ●

● Rock Springs

Fort Bridger ●

Laramie ●

● Evanston

Cheyenne ⊛

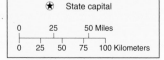

WYOMING
Political Map

⊛   State capital

0	25	50 Miles

0	25	50	75	100 Kilometers

The drawing of Wyoming on this page is called a political map. It shows features created by people, such as cities and parks. The map on the facing page is called a physical map. It shows physical features of Wyoming, such as mountains, rivers, and lakes. The colors represent a range of elevations, or heights above sea level (see legend box). This map also shows the geographical regions of Wyoming.

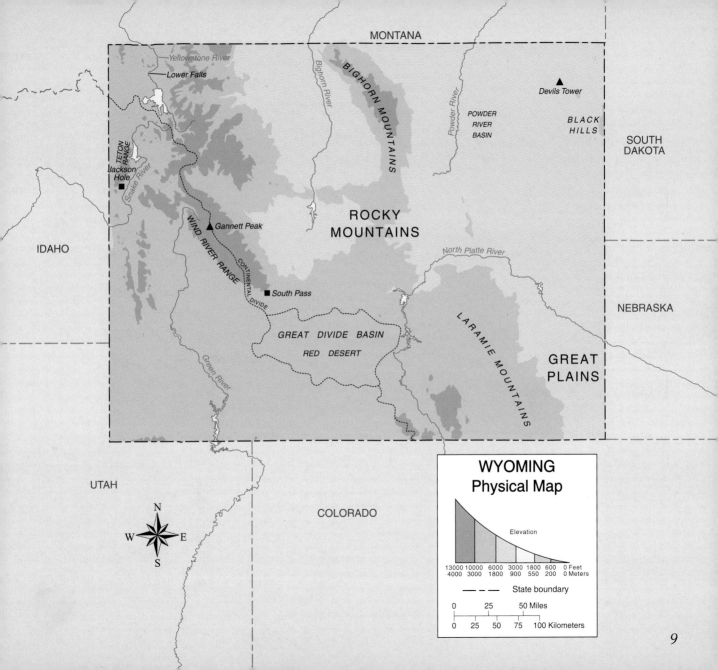

MONTANA

Yellowstone River

Lower Falls

BIGHORN MOUNTAINS

Bighorn River

Powder River

Devils Tower ▲

POWDER RIVER BASIN

BLACK HILLS

SOUTH DAKOTA

TETON RANGE

Jackson Hole ■

Snake River

▲ Gannett Peak

WIND RIVER RANGE

ROCKY MOUNTAINS

IDAHO

CONTINENTAL DIVIDE

■ South Pass

North Platte River

GREAT DIVIDE BASIN

RED DESERT

LARAMIE MOUNTAINS

NEBRASKA

GREAT PLAINS

Green River

UTAH

COLORADO

N
W E
S

WYOMING
Physical Map

Elevation

| 13000 | 10000 | 6000 | 3000 | 1800 | 600 | 0 Feet |
| 4000 | 3000 | 1800 | 900 | 550 | 200 | 0 Meters |

– – – State boundary

0   25   50 Miles

0   25   50   75   100 Kilometers

Rock formations interrupt the plains in eastern Wyoming, where the land is mostly flat.

A vast area of grassland, the Great Plains region spreads across eastern Wyoming. It is part of a flat, grassy **plateau** (highland) that stretches from Canada to Texas. The mountainous Black Hills of South Dakota spill onto the northeastern corner of Wyoming's plains. Long ridges and low, steep hills also break up the flat land. Cattle graze on the region's rich variety of grasses.

In the central part of the state, the plains meet the Rocky Mountains (or Rockies), which run north to south and cover much of central and western Wyoming. The Rocky Mountain region of Wyoming is part of a large mountain system that runs all the way from Alaska to New Mexico. In the Wind River Range, Wyoming's highest point—Gannett Peak—reaches 13,804 feet. Other major ranges include the Teton Range, the Bighorn Mountains, and the Laramie Mountains.

Some of these mountain ranges are separated by broad, dry valleys called **basins.** The basins receive so little rain that some are considered deserts. Cattle and sheep are raised in the basins. They graze on the short grasses, sagebrush, and other small plants that don't need a lot of water to grow.

The southern part of the Great Divide Basin is sometimes called the Red Desert because of its red rock.

The Yellowstone River creates waterfalls in Wyoming almost as high as New York's Niagara Falls. Lower Falls drops 308 feet.

Although much of Wyoming is very dry, the state is famous for snow-fed waterways such as the fast-flowing Yellowstone River. This waterway has carved out a spectacular canyon in Yellowstone National Park in northwestern Wyoming. Other important rivers are the Snake, the Green, the Bighorn, the Powder, and the North Platte.

Rivers in Wyoming flow to either the Atlantic Ocean or the Pacific Ocean, depending on which side of the **Continental Divide** they lie. Following a line of Rocky Mountain peaks, the divide cuts through Wyoming from its northwestern corner to the south central part of the state. The rivers on the east side of the divide flow toward the Atlantic. Those on the west flow toward the Pacific.

In general the state's climate is cool and dry. The Great Plains are usually

warmer and milder than the mountains, where temperatures can drop below freezing even in the summer. January temperatures in the northwestern mountains average an icy 12° F. On the Great Plains, the city of Casper averages a slightly milder 22° F. The average July temperature in the northwest is 59° F, while Casper enjoys 71° F.

Wyoming winters are cold and snowy.

Wildflowers, such as Indian paintbrush, come to life on Wyoming's hillsides in the spring.

Most of Wyoming's **precipitation** (rain, snow, sleet, and hail) falls in the Rockies. Each year the mountains receive about 50 inches of rain, while some basin areas get as little as 5 inches. In the winter, about 260 inches of snow cover the slopes. In contrast the basins get only 15 inches of snow each year.

Like the weather, the state's plants vary with the elevation, or height, of the land. Indian paintbrush, forget-me-nots, and other wildflowers color the mountainsides each spring. Mosses, lichens, and evergreen trees such as the lodgepole pine and Douglas fir also grow in the high forests.

Aspens and other broad-leaved trees appear at lower elevations. More than 150 kinds of grasses, such as bluegrass and redtop, thrive in the Great Plains region. Greasewood brush, yuccas, cactuses, and other plants that need little water grow in the driest areas of the state.

In some parts of Wyoming, winds blow so strongly in one direction that tree branches grow the way the wind blows.

Bison, or buffalo, once numbered in the millions on the Great Plains. In Wyoming only a few herds survive, mostly in Yellowstone National Park. The world's largest elk herds spend each winter in the National Elk Refuge at the base of the Tetons.

Grizzly bears share high wilderness areas with black bears, lynxes, and mountain lions. Pronghorn antelope and mule deer graze in the basins and on the Great Plains. Otters, gray wolves, and coyotes also make their homes in Wyoming's wilds.

Wyoming wildlife includes mountain bluebirds *(above)* and wild horses *(right)*.

THE HISTORY

The Equality State

More than 11,000 years ago, the first people came to the area of Wyoming. They were hunters in search of prey. In the mountains, the hunters found elk and mountain sheep. Bison and woolly mammoths roamed the plains.

To kill their prey, hunters drove the animals over cliffs or into sand pits. Lying wounded on the ground or stuck in the sand, the animals could be easily killed with arrows or spears. People ate the meat and used the skins for clothing and shelter. Bone and horns were made into tools.

The hunters and gatherers who came to the Wyoming area also fished in mountain streams. Those who lived in the basins gathered roots, nuts, and seeds and hunted lizards, squirrels, and rabbits.

Snowshoes allowed Plains Indian hunters to track their prey through deep snow.

By 1700, groups of American Indians, or Native Americans, were living throughout much of the Wyoming region. These descendants of the early hunters and gatherers were known as Plains Indians. The Crow and Shoshone were the largest of these groups in the area.

The abundant buffalo herds of the West were the main food for the Plains Indians. The Indians also used buffalo skins to make clothing, bedding, and shelter. They made the bones and horns into tools and weapons.

Over time other groups of Plains Indians came to the Wyoming area from the east. White settlers had forced these groups from their lands. They included the Cheyenne, the Arapaho, and the Lakota (also called Sioux). The newcomers pushed the Shoshone and Crow from the Great Plains into the Rocky Mountain region. Because there were so many different groups in the area, a common sign language developed among them.

Native Americans used animal skins for many things. They painted stories about their lives on buffalo hides, and they also made clothing from them.

During the summer, the Plains Indians left their villages in search of bison. While on the hunt, the hunters lived in tepees, which were easy to put up and take down. In the autumn, the Indians packed up their tepees and brought the yearly supply of meat back to their villages.

In the early 1700s, horses were brought north into the Wyoming region from Spanish settlements far to the south. On horseback, the Plains Indians could travel farther from their villages and kill more bison than they could on foot. Many Indians gave up village life to hunt bison year round.

Plains Indians made tepees by stretching buffalo hides over wooden poles.

Europeans first arrived in the region to search for fur-bearing animals in the mid-1700s. At that time, about 10,000 Indians lived in the Wyoming area. Most of the region was part of the Louisiana Territory, a vast area between the Mississippi River and the Rocky Mountains. France claimed the territory until 1803, when the United States bought the land in a deal called the Louisiana Purchase.

U.S. president Thomas Jefferson sent explorers Meriwether Lewis and William Clark to map the Louisiana Territory in 1804. Although they never entered Wyoming, the two men came back with tales of the West's plentiful wildlife.

Because of these stories, trappers and traders from the eastern United States and from Canada headed toward the Rockies. The adventurers hoped to get rich trapping beavers, whose furs were sold at high prices in Europe to be made into stylish hats.

Most of the Wyoming area was part of the Louisiana Purchase.

Mountain men relied on trapping and trading furs for their living.

In 1825 fur trader William Ashley held the first annual trappers' gathering on the Green River in southwestern Wyoming. The trappers, also called mountain men, told stories and played games. They also exchanged furs with traders for food, weapons, and other supplies. For the next 15 years after that, trappers returned to the Green River on that same date.

In 1834 fur traders William Sublette and Robert Campbell built Fort William, the first permanent white settlement in the area. Over the next few years, more trading posts were built. But by the early 1840s, mountain men had trapped most of the beavers in the region. Meanwhile, beaver hats were going out of style in Europe. As a result, many trappers and traders left the area.

The trading posts they left behind became important supply stations for pioneers. These travelers began crossing Wyoming in the 1840s. Many of the pioneers came from crowded areas in the eastern United States and were looking for land to farm. Pioneers headed west on the California Trail, the Oregon Trail, and the Mormon Trail. These routes all crossed the Rockies through South Pass—a break in the mountains in what later became southwestern Wyoming.

As they traveled through some of Wyoming's rocky hills on the Oregon Trail, thousands of pioneers carved their names in the rocks.

In 1848 gold was discovered in California, and the gold rush was on. At its peak in 1850, about 55,000 gold seekers made the long and difficult trip across Wyoming on their way to the gold fields. Over time, so many wagons rolled across the land that their wheels formed waist-deep ruts in the earth.

Most of the pioneer trails across the Great Plains followed rivers. Some of the waterways dried up

Westbound wagon trains *(below)* traveled about eight miles each day. In eastern Wyoming, the ruts left in the earth by heavy wagon wheels *(inset)* can still be seen.

Pioneers gathered
to cross the
Rocky Mountains
at South Pass.

during the summer, when most pioneers made the journey west. Travelers could usually carry enough water for themselves, but sometimes the oxen that pulled the wagons died of thirst.

Many oxen couldn't find enough grass to eat along the trail and starved to death. To lighten the load for the tired and hungry animals, pioneers often abandoned their belongings on the trail or left them behind at trading posts. Because the region was so dry, very few people settled in the Wyoming area.

As they drove their wagons across Indian hunting grounds, the pioneers killed wild game for food, leaving fewer animals for the Indians to hunt. The pioneers' cooking fires sometimes blazed out of control and quickly burned up the nearby prairie grasses, which bison needed to survive. They also carried smallpox and other deadly diseases to which the Indians had never before been exposed. Thousands of Indians caught these illnesses, and many died.

All these changes threatened the Indians and their way of life. Angered, they sometimes attacked wagon trains. To protect pioneers traveling along the Oregon Trail, in 1849 the U.S. government bought the trading post at Fort William. The government turned it into a military site called Fort Laramie. U.S. soldiers at the fort helped keep the pioneers safe as they traveled through the area.

Tensions rose between pioneers and Indians after gold was discovered in Montana in the early 1860s. Gold seekers followed a new route called the Bozeman Trail. This path crossed Indian hunting grounds in north central Wyoming. Groups of Sioux, led by Red Cloud, attacked many wagon trains on this trail. In response, the U.S. government built even more forts and sent additional soldiers to the area.

The Bozeman Trail became a battleground for pioneers and Indians. The trail was closed only a few years after it opened.

Finally, after many battles, the U.S. government and Sioux leaders signed a peace **treaty** in 1868. The U.S. government agreed to give up its forts. In exchange, the Indians agreed to move to **reservations,** or areas of land set aside for them to live on. The Indians also allowed a new kind of trail to be built—this one for trains.

By the time the treaty with the Indians was signed, the Union Pacific Railroad had already begun to lay tracks across what would become southern Wyoming. Many of the railroad workers were **immigrants** who came from China. The Union Pacific also hired Irish and Scandinavian laborers, as well as many Latinos.

The railroad attracted thousands of new settlers to the Wyoming area. Those who didn't lay tracks had jobs mining coal, which was used to fuel the trains. Cities and towns such as Cheyenne and Laramie sprang up almost overnight. With so many newcomers, Wyoming was named a U.S. territory in 1868. Cheyenne became the new territory's capital city.

While railroad workers built permanent stone bridges *(at left)*, trains used temporary wooden bridges *(at right)*.

Along with the expansion of Wyoming's railroads came people who wanted to hunt bison for sport. Some hunters shot their guns into bison herds right from the windows of moving trains. Most of these hunters did not want to use the bisons' meat or hides. By the late 1800s, millions of bison had been killed.

Settlers soon learned that beef cattle could live on Wyoming's plains almost as well as bison. In the 1870s and 1880s, cowboys drove huge herds from Texas to Wyoming, where the U.S. government offered free rangeland.

Ranchers branded, or burned, a special mark into the hides of their cattle. The brands helped ranchers recognize their animals among others grazing freely on the open plains.

By 1886 about 8 million cattle were grazing on the limited supply of grasses on the Great Plains. During the hot, dry summer of that year, very little grass grew. Thousands of already hungry cattle did not survive a severe winter in 1887. Some ranchers lost so many cattle that they went out of business altogether.

In 1888 the Territory of Wyoming had about 62,000 residents—enough to ask the United States government for statehood. But some Wyomingites wondered if the government would accept their **constitution,** or set of written laws. Wyoming's state constitution granted women the right to vote—a right that women in other U.S. states did not yet have.

Many of Wyoming's residents did not want to join the Union unless women could vote. They thought that allowing women the right to vote would be a good way to attract more people to Wyoming. After much discussion, the U.S. government approved the constitution, and on July 10, 1890, Wyoming became the 44th state.

A geyser in Yellowstone National Park shoots a blast of steam.

In the early 1890s, workers drilled oil wells and built an oil refinery in Casper to process the crude, or unprocessed, oil. Several years later, in 1912, a huge oil discovery near Casper gave the state's oil industry a big boost. Wyoming's role as a major oil producer had begun. Many people rushed to the state to take jobs drilling oil. Others found work in refineries where the crude oil was made into products such as kerosene and gasoline.

The gasoline was used to fuel the nation's first cars, and many vacationers began to drive to Wyoming. People came to the state from all over the world to see natural wonders such as the hot-water **geysers** in Yellowstone National Park.

The Teapot Dome Scandal

The nation's oil industry grew rapidly in the early 1900s, after cars were first built. Gasoline, an oil product, fueled the new automobiles. The U.S. government realized that gas also could fuel the ships of the U.S. Navy.

To make sure the navy would have enough gas for its ships, the U.S. government took control of three western oil fields in 1921. The oil at these sites would be saved for the navy's future use. One of these sites was the Teapot Dome oil field near Casper, Wyoming.

But some businesspeople wanted their companies to have the right to pump the oil and sell it right away. In 1922 Edward Doheny and Harry Sinclair, two rich oil executives, made a secret deal with a high-ranking government official named Albert Fall. He arranged for the two men's companies to drill for oil at two of the government's oil fields, including Teapot Dome. In exchange Fall accepted payments and livestock totaling about $400,000.

At first no one knew of the illegal arrangement. But word soon leaked out. In 1922 the U.S. Senate began investigations, which led to several trials. The process of uncovering the truth took years. Finally, in 1929, Fall was found guilty of accepting illegal payments and was sentenced to jail and had to pay a large fine. Doheny and Sinclair were ordered to pay millions of dollars to the government, and Sinclair was sent to jail for six months.

Many tourists stopped coming to Wyoming after 1929, when an economic slump called the Great Depression began. Throughout the nation, banks failed, businesses closed, and people lost their jobs. At first Wyoming's economy continued to benefit from increasing oil production. But before long, many Wyomingites found themselves out of work.

Lack of rain caused more problems for the state in the 1930s. Dams had been built across rivers to hold back water, so it could be used for **irrigation**—the process of channeling water to dry farmland. But a drought, or long dry spell, dried up some of the rivers that once fed irrigation ditches. Without rain, crops grew poorly, as did grass. Cattle and sheep that could not find enough to eat starved to death.

When the United States entered World War II in 1941, Wyoming's economy, along with the nation's, finally began to improve. During the war, the U.S. government bought much of the state's beef to feed the nation's soldiers. And Wyoming's supplies of oil and coal were needed to fuel the military's ships and tanks.

Prisoners in Their Own Land

On December 7, 1941, Japan bombed U.S. military bases at Pearl Harbor in Hawaii. The very next day, the United States declared war on Japan, entering World War II.

As a result of Pearl Harbor, fear of Japan gripped the nation. At that time, about 120,000 Japanese Americans were living on the West Coast of the United States. The U.S. government worried that these Japanese Americans would work for Japan during the war, even though most of them had been American citizens for many years. So early in 1942, the U.S. government forced these people to leave their homes and move to camps where the government could watch them carefully.

Almost 11,000 Japanese Americans were sent to Heart Mountain Relocation Center—a camp near Cody, Wyoming. Here they lived in barracks and shacks with no running water and only small stoves for heat. U.S. soldiers kept watch over the camp, which was surrounded by barbed-wire fences and bright floodlights.

Although the war ended in September 1945, families were imprisoned at Heart Mountain until December. Most went back to the West Coast, where they had to begin their lives all over again. Not until 1990 did the U.S. government apologize for the suffering it caused innocent Japanese Americans, paying those who were still alive $20,000 each for their losses.

After the war ended in 1945, Wyoming's oil and coal industries grew even more. These fuels were used to help meet the nation's increasing demands for gasoline and electricity. In the 1970s, thousands of people came from other states looking for work in Wyoming's mines and oil fields. Between 1970 and 1980, Wyoming's population increased by more than 42 percent.

Hot springs and geysers are popular with vacationers at Yellowstone National Park.

In the 1980s, the nation found cheaper sources of energy in other countries. As a result, Wyoming's mining companies lost a lot of business. Thousands of people lost their jobs and left the state.

The state bounced back in the 1990s, with an increase in coal production. Still, the people of Wyoming want to become less dependent on the changing demand for oil and coal. New businesses, including some computer manufacturers, are starting up in the state. And the tourists who flock to see Wyoming's natural wonders continue to be important to the state's economy as well.

In 1988 fires burned large parts of Yellowstone National Park. More wildflowers than usual bloomed the next spring.

But even the state's natural wonders face risks. In the summer of 1988, forest fires swept through Yellowstone National Park, burning more than one-third of the park. And in 2001, wildfires burned 900 acres in Yellowstone and 4,600 acres in Bridger-Teton National Forest.

After the fires were put out, flowers and grass sprouted again on the scorched land. Vacationers returned and photographed the park coming back to life. Wyomingites know that, like the park, they can survive hard times, too.

PEOPLE & ECONOMY

Fueling the Nation

Many young Wyomingites grow up caring for animals.

Wyoming's modern-day cowboys ride jeeps instead of horses for cattle roundups. But they are back in the saddle for the state's many rodeos. With more than 9,000 ranches and farms, and with rodeos almost every day and night from June to Labor Day, Wyoming has earned its unofficial nickname—the Cowboy State.

Wyoming has about 494,000 residents—fewer than any other state. Most are descendants of the state's first European ranchers and farmers. About 92 percent of Wyomingites are white. African Americans, many of whom can trace their roots to black soldiers who served at frontier forts in the 1800s, make up less than 1 percent of Wyoming's population. Many of the Latinos and Asian

Americans who live in the state are descendants of the early Union Pacific Railroad workers.

Native Americans make up more than 2 percent of Wyoming's population. About half of these Native Americans live and work on the Wind River Indian Reservation in western Wyoming. Each summer the Shoshone and Arapaho hold powwows, sun dances, and other traditional celebrations on the reservation.

About two-thirds of Wyoming's residents live in small towns or rural areas. The two largest cities, Cheyenne (the capital) and Casper, each have fewer than 60,000 people. Laramie, the state's third largest city, is home to just under 28,000 residents. Road signs in some towns announce populations of only 20, 17, or even as few as 3 people. But no matter where they live, the people of the Cowboy State are proud of their heritage.

Young dancers at a powwow wear beadwork and traditional costumes.

In Cheyenne crab apple trees bloom outside the state capitol building.

History buffs can walk in the pioneers' wagon ruts at Oregon Trail Ruts National Historic Landmark near Guernsey. Museums in Cheyenne, Cody, and Riverton specialize in the history and artwork of the Plains Indians. In Cody the Whitney Gallery of Western Art displays the original works of many historic western artists, such as Frederic Remington and Charles M. Russell.

Artists exhibit their work at the annual Jackson Hole Fall Arts Festival in Jackson. Each summer, nearby Teton Village hosts well-known classical musicians at the Grand Teton Music Festival. Music festivals throughout the state offer bluegrass, folk,

and cowboy music, as well as polka and jazz.
Western melodramas, in which players act out dra-
matic historical plots, draw tourists to many towns.

The Cowboy State's many rodeos are also
popular. In Cody a rodeo takes place every
night during the summer. Cheyenne's Frontier
Days celebration lasts for nine days each July. At
this well-known event, cowboys from across the
nation rope steers and ride bucking broncos and
bulls for cash prizes.

Bull riding is just
one of the events at
a Wyoming rodeo.

Rodeo Cowgirls

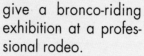

Rodeo was one of the first sports in which women competed professionally. At Cheyenne's famous Frontier Days in 1904, Bertha Kapernick was the first woman to give a bronco-riding exhibition at a professional rodeo.

Other well-known cowgirls—such as Wyoming's Prairie Rose Henderson *(top left)* and Mabel Strickland *(right)*—were famous for riding bucking broncos. Cowgirls also pleased the crowds by roping horses and steers, trick riding, and performing fancy roping stunts *(left)*.

Since the 1930s, however, cowgirls at the professional level compete in only two events—barrel racing and team roping. But cowgirls like bull-rider Tammy George and bareback-bronco rider Jan Youren hope to open these events to women. Modern cowgirls are still proving that Wyoming's most popular sport is for everyone.

Wyoming's natural wonders also draw tourists to the state. Each year more than 7 million people visit Wyoming and spend more than $1.5 billion. The most popular outdoor areas are Yellowstone National Park and Grand Teton National Park.

One popular outdoor activity in Wyoming is white-water rafting.

Visitors to the Tetons enjoy activities such as skiing, hiking, snowmobiling, and snowshoeing.

Yellowstone's famous Old Faithful geyser shoots from 3,000 to 8,000 gallons of steaming hot water into the air about every 75 minutes. In the Tetons, Jackson Hole is a popular winter ski resort area.

Wyoming's first railroad, Union Pacific, still provides jobs for many of the state's residents.

Many hotel clerks and park rangers help Wyoming's tourists to enjoy their stay. These workers have service jobs. Service workers in Wyoming also help Wyomingites buy and sell houses and land. Others work as cashiers, doctors, lawyers, and cooks.

Many service workers in Wyoming's cities and towns have jobs in banks and stores. Railroad workers help transport the state's minerals and farm products to customers all across the United States. Altogether about 58 percent of working Wyomingites have service jobs, helping other people or businesses.

WYOMING
Economic Map

The symbols on this map show where different economic activities take place in Wyoming. The legend below explains what each symbol stands for.

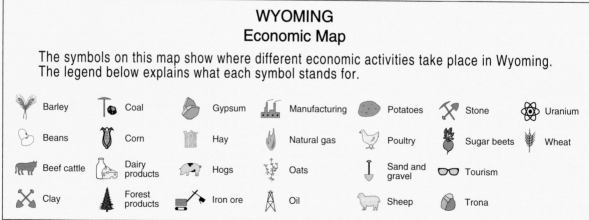

Barley	Coal	Gypsum	Manufacturing	Potatoes	Stone	Uranium
Beans	Corn	Hay	Natural gas	Poultry	Sugar beets	Wheat
Beef cattle	Dairy products	Hogs	Oats	Sand and gravel	Tourism	
Clay	Forest products	Iron ore	Oil	Sheep	Trona	

About 20 percent of Wyoming's workforce has jobs with the government. Some work at the state and local level, and some work for the U.S. government at the Francis E. Warren Air Force Base in Cheyenne.

Each year farmers in Wyoming raise about 1 million sheep.

Throughout the state, most people pay very close attention to the world's demand for oil, coal, natural gas, and other minerals. With large supplies of these fuels, Wyoming is one of the top mining states in the country. About 16,000 workers have jobs in the mining industry, which earns the state more than $1 billion each year.

About 5 percent of jobholders in Wyoming work in agriculture, which includes ranching and farming. The state has about 9,000 ranches and farms. Many of Wyoming's sheep and cattle ranchers rent some of their grazing lands from the U.S. government, which owns about half the land in the state.

Modern-day Wyoming still has enough people who make a living from ranching to deserve the nickname the Cowboy State.

Oil-drilling rigs pump oil from deep underground. Many Wyomingites are employed either mining or processing oil.

With plenty of rich grazing land, livestock do well in Wyoming. Crops need a little extra help. The state has a short growing season and less precipitation than most other states. But with irrigation, crops can grow in most parts of the state. Wyoming's major crops include hay, wheat, and barley. In some areas, farmers also grow sugar beets and beans. Every year, agriculture earns Wyoming more than $500 million.

Workers in the state's factories and processing plants know their jobs depend on Wyoming's crops and natural resources. Altogether about 4 percent of Wyoming's workers are employed in manufacturing. Refinery workers in Cheyenne, Casper, and Sinclair process crude oil. Laborers in other factories make products such as farm equipment and chemical fertilizers for crops.

49

Lumberjacks in Wyoming use horses to haul freshly cut logs *(above)*. Mills *(above left)* make the logs into lumber and other wood products.

Food processors in north central Wyoming make sugar from sugar beets grown in the area. And some of the logs from the state's forests are cut into boards at sawmills in Cheyenne and Laramie or made into pulp for paper at other plants.

Whether they are miners, ranchers, factory workers, teachers, or salesclerks, Wyomingites are proud of the contribution they make to their state.

THE ENVIRONMENT

Keeping the Water Clean

Wyoming earns more than $1 billion a year from mining the state's rich supply of minerals. One of the most valuable and abundant of these minerals is coal. In fact, Wyoming produces more than 300 million tons of coal a year—more than any other state in the nation. The coal is shipped to many different countries and 24 states, where most of it is burned at power plants to produce electricity.

Much of Wyoming's coal is mined in the Powder River Basin in the northeastern part of the state. The coal from this area contains less sulfur than coal from other regions, so it's in high demand. With less sulfur, the coal burns more cleanly and creates less air pollution.

Trains transport Wyoming's coal all across the country.

Power plants like this one convert Wyoming's coal into energy.

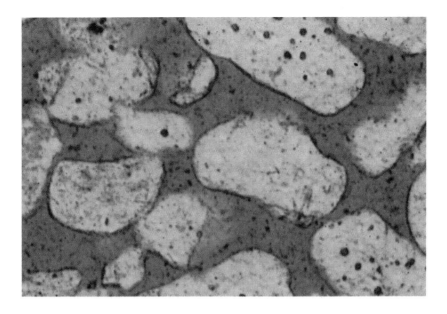

Different kinds of rocks hold groundwater. This piece of sandstone, photographed at 46 times its actual size, shows where water is stored in the large spaces between the grains of the rock.

Burning coal from the Powder River Basin may help decrease air pollution. But coal mining also affects another natural resource—**groundwater.** This water lies under the earth's surface. It is naturally stored in **aquifers,** or underground layers of rock. Many of the state's aquifers provide an important source of clean, fresh drinking water for homes and businesses. Some of Wyoming's residents worry that coal mining destroys too much of the state's groundwater.

Workers must create a giant pit to retrieve Wyoming's coal. Then, front-end loaders scoop coal into railroad cars.

In the Powder River Basin, the layers of coal serve as aquifers. Before miners dig up the coal, they first pump out water from the coal aquifers. Then, in a process called strip mining, huge bulldozers remove all the topsoil, plants, and rocky materials that cover the coal bed, creating a giant pit. Workers use explosives to blast the exposed coal bed. This breaks up the coal so that it can be easily scooped up and hauled away.

To control the coal dust created by blasting, miners regularly spray the pit with water pumped from the coal aquifer. When still more water is needed, it is pumped from aquifers that lie much deeper underground.

Each year coal-mining companies pump out millions of gallons of water from aquifers. The mining companies eventually release the water into local rivers and streams. Over time water from these waterways and from precipitation seeps back into the ground, naturally recharging (refilling) aquifers. But recharging an aquifer takes many years, especially in areas that receive very little precipitation, such as the Powder River Basin.

Open-pit coal mines, such as this one in southwestern Wyoming, are one way to get Wyoming's coal. There are about 30 open-pit coal mines in Wyoming.

Mining carries other risks for the environment. Water supplies may be depleted or contaminated by drilling or digging. Runoff from mining operations may carry chemicals or minerals that can make the water unsuitable for drinking. And sediment, or soil, from clearing trees and grass can affect the quality of the water.

Wyomingites concerned about protecting their state's water resources have formed groups such as the Powder River Basin Resource Council and the Wyoming Outdoor Council. These groups print newsletters that help people understand the issues related to mining and the environment in their state. The groups also work to convince the state of Wyoming and the U.S. government to pass tougher environmental laws and to enforce the laws that already exist.

A law passed in 1977, for example, requires coal-mining companies to reclaim, or rebuild, the land they've mined. In this process, called **reclamation**, all of the rocky materials and soil that were removed are placed back into the pit after the coal is mined.

Mining companies must reclaim the land when the mining job is finished.

Grass and trees are planted. Wells are dug to study the quality and quantity of groundwater in the area.

Sometimes mining companies use up a source of water that ranchers and other residents depended on for their homes and businesses. Mining companies are required by law to find new sources of water to replace what has been lost. This may mean tapping an aquifer that is much farther away or deeper underground. These problems can take years to fix and can make the water costly to pump.

Since the law passed, many mining companies in the state work hard to reclaim the land they have mined. And some of the money that mining companies earn each year goes toward reclaiming mines that were dug and abandoned before the 1977 law was passed.

There are ways for all people in Wyoming to protect groundwater. Residents can use less electricity, for example, so less coal will be needed to fuel electric power plants. Wyomingites who think a mining company might be breaking environmental laws can ask Wyoming's Department of Environmental Quality in Cheyenne to investigate. And in 1996, the Wyoming Department of Environmental Quality developed a plan to help Wyomingites protect and conserve their water supply.

A biologist checks the plants growing on reclaimed land.

By working together, Wyomingites can help keep their state's groundwater clean while still providing coal for the nation.

Wyoming residents hope to keep clean waters flowing into their state's future.

ALL ABOUT WYOMING

Fun Facts

In 1869 women in Wyoming became the first females in the nation to be able to vote and to hold public office. Wyomingites appointed the nation's first female judge (1870), elected the first female state legislator (1910), and elected the first female governor (1925). For these milestones, Wyoming is known as the Equality State.

With about 494,000 people, the entire state of Wyoming has fewer residents than many U.S. cities.

In 1872 Yellowstone National Park in Wyoming became the world's first national park.

Esther Morris was the country's first female judge. This statue of Morris stands outside the Wyoming state capitol in Cheyenne.

Wyoming's National Elk Refuge was created in 1912. The refuge, near Jackson, was established to protect big-game animals, such as elk and moose, even before these animals were considered endangered.

The city of Cody is named after William "Buffalo Bill" Cody. Buffalo Bill helped develop the area during the 1890s and early 1900s, influencing the construction of the Buffalo Bill Dam and other improvements.

Wyoming is famous for its rodeos. But cowboys in the state also compete in a winter event known as a sno-d-o. Here, cowboys on snowmobiles rope an iron cow pulled by another snowmobiler.

Black Thunder, in eastern Wyoming, is the largest coal mine in North and South America. Workers at the mine dig out more than 40 million tons of coal each year. Wyoming has enough coal reserves to last 500 years at the current rate of use.

STATE SONG

Wyoming's state song was officially adopted in 1955.

WYOMING

Music by G. E. Knapp; words by C. E. Winter

In the far and might - y West, Where the crim - son sun seeks rest There's a

growing splen - did State that lies a - bove On the breast of this great land; Where the

mas-sive Rock-ies stand, there's Wy - o - ming young and strong, the State I love! Wy -

o - ming, Wy - o - ming! Land of the sun - light clear! Wy - o - ming, Wy -

o - ming! Land that we hold so dear! Wy - o - ming, Wy - o - ming!

Prec - ious art thou and thine; Wy - o - ming, Wy - o - ming! Be - lov - ed State of mine!

A WYOMING RECIPE

The Cowboy State is home to rodeos, ranchers, and of course, cowboys. So it's no surprise that barbecue is a favorite food. Brush this tangy sauce on your meat and veggies for a taste of Wyoming.

COWBOY STATE BARBECUE SAUCE

You will need:

8 ounces of ketchup
2 tablespoons Worcestershire sauce
2 tablespoons prepared mustard
½ teaspoon ground pepper
½ teaspoon garlic powder

¼ teaspoon ground oregano
½ teaspoon onion powder
1 tablespoon vinegar
2 tablespoons brown sugar
½ teaspoon celery seed

1. Mix ingredients with a wire whisk. Cover.
2. Let sauce sit for one hour, to let flavors blend.
3. Add sauce to meat or veggies, then wrap in foil. Seal well.
4. Have an adult grill or cook until done. Or brush sauce over meats and vegetables near end of cooking cycle.

HISTORICAL TIMELINE

9,000 B.C.   Ancient hunters move into the Wyoming area.

A.D. 1700   Plains Indians live throughout much of Wyoming.

1803   With the Louisiana Purchase, the Wyoming region becomes part of the United States.

1825   William Ashley holds the first fur trappers gathering at Green River.

1834   William Sublette and Robert Campbell build Fort William, which later becomes Fort Laramie.

1850   The California gold rush peaks, bringing more than 50,000 pioneers across Wyoming.

1868   The United States government and Sioux leaders sign a peace treaty. Wyoming becomes a U.S. territory.

1869   Wyoming gives women the right to vote and to hold elected office.

1870   Esther H. Morris of Wyoming becomes the nation's first female judge.

1872   The U.S. Congress creates Yellowstone National Park in Wyoming.

1883 Wyoming's first oil well is drilled at Dallas Field.

1887 Wyoming ranchers lose thousands of cattle during a severe winter.

1890 Wyoming becomes the 44th state.

1910 Mary G. Bellamy of Wyoming becomes the first woman to serve as a U.S. state legislator.

1912 A large discovery of oil near Casper boosts the state's oil industry.

1922 Illegal oil drilling begins at Teapot Dome.

1925 Nellie Tayloe Ross is elected governor of Wyoming, becoming the first female governor in the United States.

1942 Japanese Americans arrive at Heart Mountain Relocation Center near Cody.

1977 Laws are passed requiring Wyoming coal-mining companies to reclaim the land they mine.

1988 Forest fires burn more than a third of Yellowstone National Park.

2001 Forest fires destroy 4,600 acres in Bridger-Teton National Forest and 900 acres in Yellowstone National Park.

OUTSTANDING WYOMINGITES

Joe Alexander

Joe Alexander (born 1943) is a world-champion rodeo star. Alexander won the professional rodeo world championship title in bareback bronco riding each year from 1971 to 1975. He was elected to the ProRodeo Hall of Fame in 1979. He is from Cora, Wyoming.

James P. Beckwourth

James P. Beckwourth (1798–1866?) was an African American fur trapper, guide, and scout. Born in Virginia, Beckwourth explored much of Wyoming for the Rocky Mountain Fur Company in the 1820s. His autobiography, *The Life and Adventures of James P. Beckwourth,* describes his life as a mountain man.

James Bridger

James Bridger (1804–1881) was a fur trapper and Rocky Mountain explorer from Virginia who became one of the best-known mountain men in the country. In 1843 he established Fort Bridger, which became a major trading post in southwestern Wyoming for pioneers heading west.

Richard Cheney (born 1941), a politician, grew up in Casper. Cheney was elected to the U.S. Congress five times and was appointed as secretary of defense. Cheney served in that role from 1989 to 1993. He was elected vice president of the United States in 2000.

Peggy Simpson Curry (1911–1987) was an author born in Scotland who eventually moved to Casper. Many of her books were about ranching and life in Wyoming. Her books include *Red Wind of Wyoming* and a novel for young readers called *A Shield of Clover.* She was often called the Poet Laureate of Wyoming.

Richard Cheney

Nancy Curtis (born 1947) is a businesswoman in Glendo, Wyoming. In 1984 she founded Wyoming's first book publishing company, High Plains Press, which publishes books about Wyoming and other parts of the western United States.

Nancy Curtis

Mike Devereaux (born 1963) is an outfielder from Casper who played for several major league baseball teams. From 1989 to 1994, Devereaux played for the Baltimore Orioles. In 1992 Devereaux batted in 107 runs, becoming the first Oriole in 12 years to drive in 100 or more runs in a season.

Mike Devereaux

Boyd H. Dowler (born 1937), a professional athlete from Cheyenne, was a leading receiver for the Green Bay Packers from 1959 to 1969. During his 11-year professional career, he caught 449 passes for a total of 6,894 yards and scored 39 touchdowns. Dowler was named to the Green Bay Packers Hall of Fame in 1978.

Boyd H. Dowler

Curt Gowdy (born 1919), a sportscaster from Green River, Wyoming, hosted a TV show called *American Sportsman* for almost 20 years. In 1984 Gowdy received the Ford C. Frick Award from the Baseball Hall of Fame.

Leonard S. Hobbs (1896–1977) was an engineer and inventor from Carbon, Wyoming. In 1952 he created an engine that could thrust a fighter plane forward at nearly 755 miles per hour. This work made passenger jet travel possible.

Harry Andrew Jackson (born 1924), a sculptor and painter, ran away to Wyoming when he was 14. The artist is best known for his painted bronze sculptures of western figures such as movie star John Wayne and Sacagawea, a Shoshone Indian guide of the 1800s. Jackson lives in Cody.

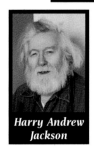
Harry Andrew Jackson

Chris LeDoux

Patricia MacLachlan

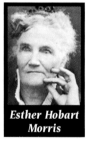

Esther Hobart Morris

Jackson Pollock

Jacques Laramie (1785?–1821) was a trapper who explored the southeastern part of Wyoming in 1819. He was the first white man to have seen and settled along the Laramie River. A Wyoming town, river, mountain range, fort, and county bear his name.

Chris LeDoux (born 1948) is a country singer, songwriter, rancher, and rodeo champion who moved to Cheyenne as a teenager. In 1976 he won the world championship title in bareback bronco riding at the National Finals Rodeo. LeDoux's songs include "I've Got to Be a Rodeo Man" and "Cadillac Ranch."

Patricia MacLachlan (born 1938), an author of children's books, was born in Cheyenne. In 1986 she won a Newbery Medal for her book *Sarah, Plain and Tall*, which was made into a television movie in 1991.

Esther Hobart Morris (1814–1902) was a politician who moved to South Pass City, Wyoming, in 1869. Less than a year later, the governor of the Territory of Wyoming appointed her to be a justice of the peace, making Morris the nation's first woman judge.

Jackson Pollock (1912–1956) was a painter born on a ranch near Cody. Considered a leader in abstract expressionist art, Pollock became famous for his painting technique. The artist would put a canvas on the floor and then use a stick or trowel—instead of a brush—to drip paint onto the canvas, forming unpredictable patterns.

Red Cloud (Mahpiua Luta) (1822–1909) was an Oglala Sioux leader born in Nebraska. Beginning in 1866, he and his followers attacked wagon trains in an effort to close the Bozeman Trail—a pioneer trail that crossed Sioux hunting grounds in northeastern

Wyoming. In 1868 the U.S. government signed a treaty agreeing to close the trail. Red Cloud is sometimes referred to as the only Native American ever to win a war against the U.S. government.

Red Cloud

Nellie Tayloe Ross (1876–1977), the nation's first female governor, moved to Cheyenne with her husband in 1902. In 1925 she was elected to complete her husband's term as governor of Wyoming after he died in office. In 1933 Ross went on to become the first female director of the U.S. Mint.

Nellie Tayloe Ross

Alan K. Simpson (born 1931) is a politician who grew up in Cody. Simpson served as a Wyoming senator from 1979 to 1997. Considered a colorful and opinionated political leader, he became director of the Institute of Politics at Harvard after retiring from politics.

Spotted Tail (1833–81) was a Sioux chief born near Fort Laramie. A capable warrior and leader, Spotted Tail supported efforts to make peace with pioneers. His talent for compromise kept his tribe out of battle many times.

Alan K. Simpson

Elinore Pruitt Stewart (1876–1933) was a writer who owned a ranch near Burntfork, Wyoming. She wrote about her life in *Letters of a Woman Homesteader*, which was made into a movie in 1979.

Washakie (1804?–1900) was a Shoshone leader who spent much of his life in Wyoming. Washakie and his people helped the U.S. Army and pioneers heading west in the mid-1800s. Washakie became the first Native American leader to be buried with U.S. military honors.

Washakie

FACTS-AT-A-GLANCE

Nickname: Equality State (official)

Song: "Wyoming" (official)

Motto: Equal Rights

Flower: Indian paintbrush

Tree: cottonwood

Bird: meadowlark

Mammal: bison

Gemstone: jade (nephrite)

Reptile: horned toad

Fish: cutthroat trout

Fossil: knightia

Dinosaur: triceratops

Date and ranking of statehood:
    July 10, 1890, the 44th state

Capital: Cheyenne

Area: 97,105 square miles

Rank in area, nationwide: 9th

Average January temperature: 19° F

Average July temperature: 67° F

Wyoming's state flag features a buffalo branded with the state seal. The woman in the center of the seal symbolizes women's rights. The rancher and the miner stand for Wyoming's major economic products—cattle and minerals.

POPULATION GROWTH

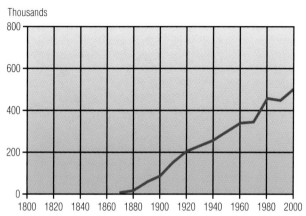

This chart shows how Wyoming's population has changed from 1870 to 2000.

The Wyoming state seal was adopted in 1893. The state motto and the woman in the center represent equality. The state's economy, agriculture, and minerals are represented by the cowboy and the miner.

Population: 493,782 (2000 census)

Rank in population, nationwide: 50th

Major cities and populations: (2000 census) Cheyenne (53,011), Casper (49,644), Laramie (27,204), Gillette (19,646), Rock Springs (18,708)

U.S. senators: 2

U.S. representatives: 1

Electoral votes: 3

Natural resources: agate, bentonite, coal, forests, gold, grazing land, gypsum, jade, limestone, natural gas, petroleum, sand and gravel, trona, uranium

Agricultural products: barley, beans, beef cattle, corn, hay, milk, oats, potatoes, sheep, sugar beets, wheat, wool

Manufactured goods: chemicals, dairy products, food products, machinery, newspapers and printed materials, petroleum products, wood products

WHERE WYOMINGITES WORK

Services—58 percent (services includes jobs in trade; community, social, and personal services; finance, insurance, and real estate; transportation, communication, and utilities)

Government—20 percent

Construction—7 percent

Mining—6 percent

Agriculture—5 percent

Manufacturing—4 percent

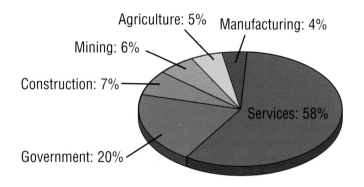

GROSS STATE PRODUCT

Services—43 percent

Mining—32 percent

Government—12 percent

Manufacturing—7 percent

Construction—4 percent

Agriculture—2 percent

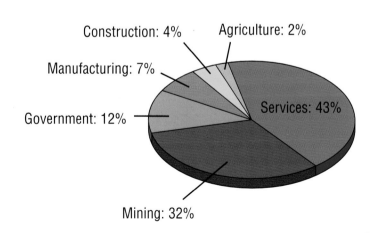

WYOMING WILDLIFE

Mammals: beaver, bison, black bear, black-footed ferret, brown bear, coyote, elk, fox, gray wolf, grizzly bear, horse, lynx, marten, moose, mountain lion, mule deer, otter, pronghorn antelope, raccoon, skunk, wildcat

Birds: bald eagle, brown pelican, duck, geese, golden eagle, grouse, mountain bluebird, pheasant, prairie falcon, sage hen, sandhill crane, wild turkey

Amphibians and reptiles: horned lizard, horned toad, ornate box turtle, rattlesnake, tiger salamander, Western toad

Fish: burbot, chub, goldeye, Plains minnow, quillback, red shiner, sand shiner, sauger, trout

Trees: aspen, cottonwood, Douglas fir, Engelmann spruce, lodgepole pine, ponderosa pine, subalpine fir

Wild plants: arnica, bluegrass, buttercup, cactus, evening star, five-finger, flax, forget-me-not, goldenrod, greasewood brush, Indian paintbrush, red top, sagebrush, saxifrage, sour dock, tufted fescues, wheat grass, windflower, yucca

Each winter, Wyoming's National Elk Refuge is home to the world's largest elk herds.

PLACES TO VISIT

Buffalo Bill Historical Center, Cody
This center features a four-museum complex, including the Whitney Gallery of Western Art, the Buffalo Bill Museum, the Plains Indian Museum, and the Cody Firearms Museum.

Devils Tower National Monument, northeastern Wyoming
Established in 1906 as the nation's first national monument, Devils Tower is a 1,267-foot volcanic column. Visitors here can hike, climb, and see a prairie dog town.

Fort Bridger State Historic Site, Fort Bridger
This site features restored buildings from the fort's military period, a reconstruction of the trading post operated by Jim Bridger, and a museum.

Fort Laramie National Historic Site, near Fort Laramie
Learn more about pioneer history at this historic fort, which was established as a trading center and later turned into a military post.

Fossil Butte National Monument, near Kemmerer
Visitors can see the fossilized remains of 50-million-year-old fish, insects, birds, reptiles, and plants at this national monument. The site features more than 75 fossils on display.

Grand Teton National Park, near Jackson
The 500-square-mile Grand Teton National Park is home to the Teton Mountains. Visitors can ski at Jackson Hole resort, camp on the shores of a mountain lake, or watch the local wildlife.

Register Cliff, near Guernsey
See where pioneers camping at the base of the cliff carved their names into the soft sandstone more than 100 years ago.

Wyoming Dinosaur Center, Thermopolis
Visitors to the Dinosaur Center can check out a dinosaur museum, tour dig sites, or dig for a day there.

Wyoming State Museum, Cheyenne
Learn about Wyoming's history, from dinosaurs to the Wild West, through exhibits and a hands-on history room.

Yellowstone National Park
The world's oldest national park features waterfalls, canyons, and geysers, including world-famous Old Faithful.

The mysterious-looking Devils Tower draws visitors to northeastern Wyoming.

ANNUAL EVENTS

Cutter Races, Jackson—*February*

High Plains Country Music Festival, Douglas—*April*

Cody Wild West Days, Cody—*May*

Plains Indian Powwow, Cody—*June*

Frontier Days, Cheyenne—*July*

Yellowstone Jazz Festival, Yellowstone National Park—*July*

Grand Teton Music Festival, Jackson Hole—*June–August*

Wyoming State Fair & Rodeo, Douglas—*August*

Cowboy Days, Evanston—*September*

Cheyenne Christmas Parade, Cheyenne—*November*

Mountains tower over glassy lakes in western Wyoming.

LEARN MORE ABOUT WYOMING

BOOKS

General

Baldwin, Guy. *Wyoming.* New York: Marshall Cavendish, 1999. For older readers.

Kent, Deborah. *Wyoming.* New York: Children's Press, 2000.

Special Interest

Freedman, Russell. *Buffalo Hunt.* New York: Holiday House, 1995. With reproductions of paintings and drawings by artists in the 1800s, this book describes how the Plains Indians relied on North American bison.

Freedman, Russell. *Cowboys of the Wild West.* New York: Clarion Books, 1990. Learn more about the duties and day-to-day life of the cowboys who worked in the West from the 1860s to the 1890s.

Klausmeier, Robert. *Cowboy.* Minneapolis, MN: Lerner Publications Company, 1996. Journey into the American past, when buffalo rumbled across the plains, prairie grass stretched for thousands of miles, and your bed might be a horse blanket under the stars.

Lazar, Jerry. *Red Cloud: Sioux War Chief.* New York: Chelsea House, 1995. This biography covers the life of the Native American leader Red Cloud.

Stone, Lynn M. *Grizzlies.* Minneapolis: Carolrhoda Books, Inc., 1993. Learn more about these threatened animals that make their home in Wyoming's wilderness.

Terry, Michael Bad Hand. *Daily Life in a Plains Indian Village, 1868.* New York: Clarion Books, 1999. Readers learn how Cheyenne Indians lived in 1868, before European settlement forced them onto reservations. The text covers topics such as housing, food, warfare, medicine, and government.

Welch, Catherine A. *Children of the Relocation Camps.* Minneapolis, MN: Carolrhoda Books, Inc., 1999. With photographs from the era, this book looks at how Japanese American children left their lives behind and courageously faced the injustice of relocation camps during World War II.

Fiction

Ehrlich, Gretchen. *A Blizzard Year: Timmy's Almanac of Seasons.* Westport, CT: Hyperion Press, 1999. After a blizzard kills their livestock, Timmy and her family may lose the family ranch.

Roberts, Willo Davis. *The Absolutely True Story: How I Visited Yellowstone Park with the Terrible Rupes.* New York: Atheneum, 1994. Twelve-year-old Lewis and his sister Alison travel to Yellowstone with their next door neighbors the Rupes. But their dream vacation soon turns sour.

Wallace, Bill. *Red Dog.* New York: Holiday House, 1987. In Wyoming Territory in the 1860s, young Adam faces danger and adventure as he tries to save his family from kidnappers.

WEBSITES

Welcome to The State of Wyoming
<http://www.state.wy.us/>
Visit the state's official website to learn more about government, history, and business in the Equality State. The site also includes links to important websites.

Travel & Tourism in Wyoming
<http://www.wyomingtourism.org/tourism/index.cfm>
Find places to visit and things to do in Wyoming. The website includes an interactive visitor center.

Wyoming Tribune-Eagle Online
<http://www.wyomingnews.com/>
Get national, local, and feature news stories with this online version of the capital city's newspaper.

PRONUNCIATION GUIDE

Arapaho (uh-RAP-uh-hoh)

Cheyenne (shy-AN)

Cody (KOH-dee)

Guernsey (GURN-zee)

Lakota (luh-KOH-tuh)

Laramie (LEHR-uh-mee)

Platte (PLAT)

Shoshone (shuh-SHOH-nay)

Sioux (SOO)

Teton (TEE-tahn)

Wyoming often brings to mind images of rural life—and Wyomingites like it that way. Only one-third of the population lives in big cities.

GLOSSARY

aquifer: an underground layer of rock, sand, or gravel containing water that can be drawn out for use above ground

basin: a bowl-shaped region; all the land drained by a river and its branches

constitution: the system of basic laws or rules of a government, society, or organization; the document in which these laws or rules are written

continental divide: a line of elevated land that determines the direction the rivers of a continent flow. In North America, the line is sometimes called the Great Divide. The Rocky Mountains mark the North American divide, separating rivers that flow east from those that flow west.

geyser: an underground spring heated by hot rocks. The spring periodically throws a jet of hot water and steam into the air through a hole in the ground.

groundwater: water that lies beneath the earth's surface. The water comes from rain and snow that seep through soil into the cracks and other openings in rocks. Groundwater supplies wells and springs.

immigrant: a person who moves into a foreign country and settles there

irrigation: a method of watering land by directing water through canals, ditches, pipes, or sprinklers

plateau: a large, relatively flat area that stands above the surrounding land

precipitation: rain, snow, and other forms of moisture that fall to earth

reclamation: the process of rebuilding land and making it usable again for plants, animals, or people

reservation: public land set aside by the government to be used by Native Americans

treaty: an agreement between two or more groups, usually having to do with peace or trade

INDEX

PHOTO ACKNOWLEDGMENTS

Cover photographs by © Bill Ross/CORBIS (left) and © Tom Brakefield/CORBIS (right); PresentationMaps.com, pp. 1, 8, 9, 46; © Pat O'Hara/CORBIS, pp. 2–3; © Swift/Vanuga Images/CORBIS, p. 3; © Ken Lucas/Visuals Unlimited, pp. 4 (detail), 7 (detail), 17 (detail), 38 (detail), 51 (detail); © Daniel D. Lamoreux/ Visuals Unlimited, p. 6; © Wolfgang Kaehler, pp. 7, 36; Jeff Vanuga, pp. 10, 11, 14, 16 (bottom), 24 (inset), 39, 47, 48, 50 (top); Robert Czarnomski, pp. 12, 38; Kent & Donna Dannen, pp. 13, 15; © Adam Jones, pp. 16 (top), 76; IPS, pp. 18, 19; Wyoming State Archives, pp. 20, 30, 32, 33, 42 (bottom left), 69 (second from top); Denver Public Library, Western History Department, pp. 22, 24 (bottom), 68 (second from bottom); Robert Tyszka, pp. 23, 45, 54, 60, 74; American Heritage Center, University of Wyoming, pp. 25, 42 (top left and right); University of Michigan Museum of Art, Bequest of Henry C. Lewis, 1895.80, p. 27; Oakland Museum History Dept., p. 29; Buffalo Bill Historical Center, Cody, WY, Jack Richard Collection, P.89.1428, p. 35; Domenica DiPiazza, p. 37; Tom Dietrich, pp. 40, 41, 43, 50 (bottom), 80; C. W. Biedel, M.D./Laatsch-Hupp Photo, p. 44; Wyoming Division of Tourism, p. 49; © Scott T. Smith, pp. 51, 52, 55, 57, 58; American Assoc. of Petroleum Geologists, p. 53; © Buddy Mays/Travel Stock, p. 59; Jack Lindstrom, p. 61; Tim Seeley, pp. 63, 71 (top), 72; Pro Rodeo Hall of Fame, p. 66 (top); Utah State Historical Society, p. 66 (second from top and second from bottom); Reuters NewMedia Inc./CORBIS, p. 66 (bottom); Dove Studio, p. 67 (top); Mort Tadder/Baltimore Orioles, p. 67 (second from top); Green Bay Packers, p. 67 (second from bottom); Harry Jackson Studios, p. 67 (bottom); Butch Adams, p. 68 (top); Anne MacLachlan, p. 68 (second from top); Jackson Pollock Papers, Archives of American Art, Smithsonian Institution, p. 68 (bottom); Office of Senator Alan Simpson, p. 69 (second from bottom); *Dictionary of American Portraits*, p. 69 (top, bottom); Jean Matheny, p. 70; USDA/Ron Nichols, p. 73.